NOTES TO USERS

THIS publication is divided into five parts: Descriptive, Handling, Operating Data, Emergencies, and Illustrations. Part I gives only a brief description of the controls with which the pilot should be acquainted.

These Notes are complementary to A.P. 2095 Pilot's Notes General and assume a thorough knowledge of its contents. All pilots should be in possession of a copy of A.P. 2095 (see A.M.O. A93/43).

Words in capital letters indicate the actual markings on the controls concerned.

Additional copies may be obtained by the Station Publications Officer by application on Form 294A, in duplicate, to Command headquarters for onward transmission to A.P.F.S., 81 Fulham Road, S.W.3 (see A.M.O. A. 1114/44). The number of this publication must be quoted in full—A.P. 1565J, P & L —P.N.

Comments and suggestions should be forwarded through the usual channels to the Air Ministry (D.T.F.).

SPITFIRE F. IX, XI & XVI

AIR MINISTRY
September 1946
(*Reprinted—February* 1947)

AIR PUBLICATION 1565J, P & L—P.N.
Pilot's Notes
3rd Edition

SPITFIRE IX, XI & XVI PILOT'S NOTES

3rd Edition. *This Edition supersedes all previous issues.*

LIST OF CONTENTS

PART I—DESCRIPTIVE

	Para.
INTRODUCTION	1

FUEL, OIL AND COOLANT SYSTEMS

Fuel tanks	2
Fuel cocks	3
Fuel pumps	4
Fuel contents gauges and pressure warning light	5
Oil system	6
Engine coolant system	7
Intercooler system	8

MAIN SERVICES

Hydraulic system	9
Electrical system	10
Pneumatic system	11

AIRCRAFT CONTROLS

Trimming tabs	12
Undercarriage control	13
Undercarriage indicators	14
Undercarriage warning horn	15
Flaps control	16
Wheel brakes	17
Flying controls locking gear	18

ENGINE CONTROLS *Para.*

    Throttle 19
    Propeller control 20
    Supercharger controls 21
    Intercooler protector 22
    Radiator flap control 23
    Slow-running cut-out 24
    Idle cut-off control 25
    Carburettor air intake filter control 26
    Cylinder priming pump 27
    Ignition switches and starter buttons 28
    Ground battery starting 29

OTHER CONTROLS

    Cockpit door 30
    Sliding hood controls 31
    Signal discharger 32

PART II—HANDLING

Management of the fuel system 33
Preliminaries 34
Starting the engine and warming up (Merlin 61 and 63 engines) 35
Starting the engine and warming up (Merlin 66, 70 and 266 engines) 36
Testing the engine and services 37
Check list before take-off 38
Take-off 39
Climbing 40
General flying 41
Stalling 42
Spinning 43
Diving 44
Aerobatics 45
Check list before landing 46
Approach and landing 47
Mislanding 48
Beam approach 49
After landing 50

PART III—OPERATING DATA *Para.*

Engine data—Merlins 61, 63, 66, 70 and 266	51
Flying limitations	52
Position error corrections	53
Maximum performance	54
Economical flying	55
Fuel capacities and consumption	56

PART IV—EMERGENCIES

Undercarriage emergency operation	57
Failure of the pneumatic system	58
Hood jettisoning	59
Forced landing	60
Ditching	61
Crowbar	62

PART V—ILLUSTRATIONS *Fig.*

Instrument panel	1
Cockpit—port side	2
Cockpit—starboard side	3
Fuel system diagram	4

AIR PUBLICATION 1565J, P & L—P.N.
Pilot's Notes

PART I

DESCRIPTIVE

NOTE.—The numbers quoted in brackets after items in the text refer to key numbers of the illustrations in Part V.

INTRODUCTION

1. (i) The variants of the Spitfire IX, XI and XVI are distinguished by prefix letters denoting the general operating altitude or role and the suffix letter (e) is used where ·5-in. guns replace ·303-in. guns. The aircraft are all essentially similar, but the following table shows the main features that give the various versions their distinguishing letters:

F IX	Merlin 61, 63 or 63A; two 20-mm. and four ·303-in. guns.
LF IX	Merlin 66; two 20-mm. and four ·303-in. guns.
LF IX (e)	Merlin 66; two 20-mm. and two ·5-in. guns.
HF IX	Merlin 70; two 20-mm. and four ·303-in. guns.
HF IX (e)	Merlin 70; two 20-mm. and two ·5-in. guns.
PR XI	Merlin 61, 63, 63A or 70.
F XVI	Merlin 266; two 20-mm. and two ·5-in. guns.

(ii) Merlin 61 and 63 engines have S.U. float-type carburettors, but on Merlin 66, 70 and 266 engines these are replaced by Bendix-Stromberg injection carburettors.

(iii) All these marks of aircraft are fitted with Rotol 4-bladed hydraulic propellers and on the majority of the aircraft the wing tips are clipped.

(iv) Later Mk. IX and XVIs have "rear view" fuselages which incorporate "tear-drop" sliding hoods.

PART I—DESCRIPTIVE

FUEL, OIL AND COOLANT SYSTEMS

2. **Fuel tanks** (see Fig. 4).—Fuel is carried in two tanks mounted one above the other (the lower one is self-sealing) forward of the cockpit. The top tank feeds into the bottom tank and fuel is delivered to the carburettor, through a filter, by an engine-driven pump. On Merlin 61 and 63 engine installations there is a fuel cooler, while on Bendix-Stromberg carburettor installations a de-aerator in the carburettor, for separating accumulated air from the fuel, is vented to the top tank. Later Mk. IX and all F. Mk. XVI aircraft mount two additional fuel tanks with a combined capacity of 75 gallons (66 gallons in aircraft with "rear view" fuselages); they are fitted in the fuselage behind the cockpit. These tanks should only be filled for special operations at the discretion of the appropriate Area Commander and normally their cocks should be wired OFF. If fitted in aircraft with "rear view" fuselages, they must not be used in any circumstances.

A.L.1
Part I
para. 2

The capacities of the main tanks are as follows :

Top tank	48 gallons
Bottom tank	37 gallons or 47* gallons
Total	85 gallons or 95* gallons

* On some aircraft; generally those with "rear-view" fuselages.

On PR XI aircraft there is a 66-gal. tank in each wing, bringing the total capacity up to 217 gal. These tanks feed the engine direct by gravity and the cocks are controlled by the two levers (red and green) fitted on the left-hand side below the rudder trim control. A contents gauge for the port tank is on the left-hand side and one for the starboard tank is high up on the right-hand side of the instrument panel.

An auxiliary "blister" drop tank of 30, 45 or 90-gal. capacity (on the PR XI, of 170 gal.) can be fitted under the fuselage; these tanks feed the engine direct and do not replenish the main tanks. To meet the possibility of engine cutting due to fuel boiling in warm weather at high altitudes, the main tanks are pressurised; pressurising, however, impairs the self-sealing properties of the tanks and should be turned OFF if a tank is holed.

3. **Fuel cocks.**—The cock control for the main tanks is a lever (47) fitted below the engine starting pushbuttons

PART I—DESCRIPTIVE

and the pressurising control (50) is below the right-hand side of the instrument panel. The cock control (58) and jettison lever (59) for the auxiliary drop tank are mounted together on the right-hand side of the cockpit, below the undercarriage control unit. The jettison lever is pulled up to jettison the drop tank, but cannot be operated until the cock control is moved forward to the OFF position. The cock for the rear fuselage tanks (when fitted) is to the left of the seat.

4. **Fuel pumps.**—On Bendix-Stromberg carburettor installations an electric booster pump, operated by a switch on the left-hand side of the cockpit, is fitted in the lower main tank. On early aircraft this pump is not fitted, but a hand wobble pump is provided instead, just forward of the remote contactor.

   NOTE.—On aircraft which have rear fuselage tanks a second pump is fitted (in the lower rear tank) and the control switch described above then has three positions.

5. **Fuel contents gauges and pressure warning light.**—The contents gauge (19) on the right-hand side of the instrument panel indicates the quantity of fuel in the lower main tank when the adjacent pushbutton is depressed. On aircraft with rear fuselage tanks a gauge (for the lower rear tank only) is mounted beside the main tanks' gauge. This also operates when the main tanks' gauge pushbutton is depressed. On later L.F. Mk. XVI aircraft the two gauges are mounted together, the left-hand dial (which is calibrated only up to 50 gallons) indicating the contents of the main tanks.

   The fuel pressure warning light (18) is operative when the switch (34) on the throttle quadrant is on and comes on at any time when fuel pressure at the carburettor falls appreciably below normal.

6. **Oil system.**—Oil is supplied by a tank of 7·5 gallons oil capacity under the engine mounting, which is pressurised to 2½ lb./sq.in., and passes through a filter before entering the engine. An oil cooler is fitted in the underside

8

PART I—DESCRIPTIVE

of the port wing and oil pressure (20) and temperature (17) gauges are fitted on the instrument panel. When carrying an auxiliary drop tank of 170 gallons capacity a larger oil tank of either 8·5 or 14·5 gallons capacity must be fitted.

7. **Engine coolant system.**—On early aircraft only, circulation of the coolant through the underwing radiators is thermostatically controlled, the radiators being by-passed until the coolant reaches a certain temperature. The header tank is mounted above the reduction gear casing and is fitted with a relief valve. On all aircraft the radiator flaps are fully automatic and are designed to open at a coolant temperature of 115° C. A pushbutton is fitted on the electrical panel for ground testing, and there is a coolant temperature gauge (16) on the instrument panel.

8. **Intercooler system.**—On all aircraft the high temperatures resulting from two-stage supercharging necessitate the introduction of an intercooler between the supercharger delivery and the induction manifolds, particularly when S (high) gear is used. An auxiliary pump passes the coolant from a separate header tank to a radiator under the starboard wing, and thence through the supercharger casing to the intercooler, where the charge is cooled by loss of heat passing to the coolant. On early aircraft a thermostatically operated switch in the induction pipe is connected to the supercharger operating ram and causes it to change the supercharger to M (low) gear in the event of the charge temperature becoming excessive. This change of gear ratio is indicated to the pilot by a pushbutton, which springs out on the instrument panel. The supercharger will change back to high gear after the temperature of the charge has returned to normal and the pushbutton has been pushed in. If, however, the excessive temperature is of a permanent nature, due to failure of the intercooler system, the pushbutton will continue to spring out and the flight should be continued in low gear.

MAIN SERVICES

9. **Hydraulic system.**—Oil is carried in a reservoir on the fireproof bulkhead and passes through a filter to an engine-driven pump for operation of the undercarriage.

PART I—DESCRIPTIVE

10. **Electrical system.**—A 12-volt generator supplies an accumulator which in turn supplies the whole of the electrical installation. A voltmeter (10) across the accumulator is fitted at the top of the instrument panel and a red light (40), on the electrical panel, marked POWER FAILURE, is illuminated when the generator is not delivering current to the accumulator.

    NOTE.—If the electrical system fails or is damaged, the supercharger will be fixed in low gear and the radiator flaps will remain closed.

11. **Pneumatic system.**—An engine-driven air compressor charges two storage cylinders to a pressure of 300 lb./sq.in. for operation of the flaps, radiator flaps, supercharger ram, brakes and guns.

    NOTE.—If the pneumatic system fails, the supercharger will be fixed in low gear, but the position of the radiator flaps will depend on the nature of the failure.

AIRCRAFT CONTROLS

12. **Trimming tabs.**—The elevator trimming tabs are controlled by a handwheel (30) on the left-hand side of the cockpit, the indicator (24) being on the instrument panel. The rudder trimming tab is controlled by a small handwheel (27) and is not provided with an indicator. The aircraft tends to turn to starboard when the handwheel is rotated clockwise.

13. **Undercarriage control.**—The undercarriage selector lever (52) moves in a gated quadrant on the right-hand side of the cockpit.

    To raise the undercarriage the lever must be moved downwards and inwards to disengage it from the gate, and then moved forward smartly in one movement to the full extent of the quadrant. When the undercarriage is locked up the lever will automatically spring into the forward gate.

    To lower the undercarriage the lever must be held forward for about two seconds, then pulled back in one

PART I—DESCRIPTIVE

movement to the full extent of the quadrant. When the undercarriage is locked down the lever will spring into the rear gate.

Warning.—The lever must never be moved into either gate by hand as this will cut off the hydraulic pressure.

An indicator in the quadrant shows DOWN, IDLE or UP depending on the position of the hydraulic valve. UP and DOWN should show only during the corresponding operation of the undercarriage and IDLE when the lever is in either gate. If, when the engine is not running, the indicator shows DOWN, it should return to IDLE when the engine is started; if it does not, probable failure of the hydraulic pump is indicated.

14. **Undercarriage indicators**

    (*a*) *Electrical visual indicator.*—The electrically operated visual indicator (2) has two semi-transparent windows on which the words UP on a red background and DOWN on a green background are lettered; the words are illuminated according to the position of the undercarriage. The switch (34) for the DOWN circuit is moved to the on position by a striker on the throttle lever as the throttle is opened.

    (*b*) *Mechanical position indicators.*—On early aircraft a rod that extends through the top surface of the main plane is fitted to each undercarriage unit. When the wheels are down the rods protrude through the top of the main planes and when they are up, the tops of the rods, which are painted red, are flush with the main plane surfaces.

15. **Undercarriage warning horn.**—The horn, fitted in early aircraft only, sounds when the throttle lever is nearly closed and the undercarriage is not lowered. It cannot be silenced until the throttle is opened again or the undercarriage is lowered.

16. **Flaps control.**—The split flaps have two positions only, up and fully down. They are controlled by a finger lever (5) on the instrument panel.

PART I—DESCRIPTIVE

17. **Wheel brakes.**—The brake lever is fitted on the control column spade grip and a catch for retaining it in the on position for parking is fitted below the lever pivot. A triple pressure gauge (25), showing the air pressures in the pneumatic system cylinders and at each brake, is mounted on the instrument panel.

18. **Flying controls locking gear.**—Two struts are stowed on the right-hand side of the cockpit aft of the seat. The longer strut and the arm attached to it lock the control column to the seat and to the starboard datum longeron, and the shorter strut, attached to the other strut by a cable, locks the rudder pedals. The controls should be locked with the seat in its highest position.

ENGINE CONTROLS

19. **Throttle.**—The throttle lever (33) is gated at the climbing boost position. There is a friction adjuster (31) on the side of the quadrant. The mixture control is automatic and there is no pilot's control lever.

20. **Propeller control**
   (i) On early aircraft the speed control lever (35) on the inboard side of the throttle quadrant varies the governed r.p.m. from 3,000 down to 1,800.
   (ii) On later aircraft the propeller speed control is interconnected with the throttle control. The inter-connection is effected by a lever, similar to the normal speed control lever, which is known as the override lever. When this is pulled back to the stop in the quadrant (the AUTOMATIC position) the r.p.m. are controlled by the positioning of the throttle lever. When pushed fully forward to the MAX. R.P.M. position it overrides the interconnection device and r.p.m. are then governed at approximately 3,000. The override lever can be used in the same way as the conventional propeller speed control lever to enable the pilot to select higher r.p.m. than those given by the interconnection.

   It must be remembered that the interconnection is effected only when the override lever is pulled back to

PART I—DESCRIPTIVE

the stop in the quadrant; indiscriminate use of the lever in any position forward of this stop will increase fuel consumption considerably.

At low altitudes (and at altitudes just above that at which high gear is automatically engaged) the corresponding r.p.m. for a given boost with the override lever set to AUTOMATIC are as follows:

Boost (lb./sq.in.)	*R.P.M.*
Below $+3$	1,800–1,850
At $+7$	2,270–2,370
At $+12$ (at the gate)	2,800–2,900
At $+18$ (throttle fully open)	3,000–3,050

(iii) A friction damping control (46) is fitted on the inboard side of the throttle quadrant.

21. **Supercharger controls.**—The two-speed two-stage supercharger automatically changes to high gear at about 21,000 feet (14,000 feet on Merlin 66 and 11,000 feet on Merlin 266 installations) on the climb and back to low gear at about 19,000 feet (12,500 feet on Merlin 66 and 10,000 feet on Merlin 266 installations) on the descent. An override switch is fitted on the instrument panel by means of which low gear may be selected at any height. There is a pushbutton (42) on the electrical panel for testing the gear change on the ground, and a red light (13) on the instrument panel comes on when high-gear is engaged, on the ground or in flight.

22. **Intercooler protector.**—See para. 8 and note. On early aircraft, should excessive charge temperatures cause the pushbutton (15) to spring out, it may be reset manually to allow the supercharger to return to high gear; it will, however, only remain in if the charge temperature has returned to normal.

23. **Radiator flap control.**—The radiator flaps are fully automatic and there is no manual control. A pushbutton (41) for testing the radiator flaps is on the electrical panel.

24. **Slow-running cut-out (Merlin 61 and 63 installations only).**—The control on the carburettor is operated by pulling the ring (37) below the left-hand side of the instrument panel.

PART I—DESCRIPTIVE

25. **Idle cut-off control (Merlin 66, 70 and 266 installations only).**—The idle cut-off valve on Bendix-Stromberg carburettors is operated by moving the short lever on the throttle quadrant through the gate to the fully aft position. On early Stromberg carburettor installations this lever is not fitted, but the cut-off valve is operated by the ring (37) which on other aircraft operates the slow-running cut-out.

    NOTE.—The idle cut-off control must be in the fully aft position, or cut-off position, at all times when a booster pump is on and the engine is not running; otherwise, fuel will be injected into the supercharger at high pressure and there will be, in consequence, a serious risk of fire.

26. **Carburettor air intake filter control**

    On tropicalised aircraft the carburettor air intake filter control on the left-hand side of the cockpit has two positions OPEN and CLOSED (NORMAL INTAKE and FILTER IN OPERATION on later aircraft). The CLOSED (or FILTER IN OPERATION) position must be used for all ground running, take-off and landing and when flying in sandy or dust-laden conditions.

    NOTE.— (i) In the air it may be necessary to reduce speed to 200 m.p.h. I.A.S. or less, before the filter control lever can be operated.

    (ii) The filter control lever must always be moved slowly.

27. **Cylinder priming pump.**—A hand-operated pump (48) for priming the engine is fitted below the right-hand side of the instrument panel.

28. **Ignition switches and starter buttons.**—The ignition switches (1) are on the left-hand side of the instrument panel and the booster-coil (22) and the engine starter (21) pushbuttons immediately below it. Each pushbutton is covered by a safety shield.

29. **Ground battery starting.**—The socket for starting from an external supply is mounted on the starboard engine bearer.

PART I—DESCRIPTIVE

OTHER CONTROLS

30. **Cockpit door.**—The cockpit door is fitted with a two-position catch which allows it to be partly opened, thus preventing the sliding hood from coming forward in the event of a crash or forced landing. It will be found that the catch operates more easily when the aircraft is airborne than when on the ground.

    NOTE.—On aircraft with "tear-drop" hoods, the two-position catch should not be used.

31. **Sliding hood controls**
    (i) On later Mk. IX and XVI aircraft the "tear-drop" hood is opened and closed by a crank handle mounted on the right-hand cockpit wall, above the undercarriage selector lever. The handle must be pulled inwards before it can be rotated. The hood may be locked in any intermediate position by releasing the crank handle which then engages with the locking ratchet.

    (ii) From outside the cockpit the hood may be opened and closed by hand provided the pushbutton below the starboard hood rail is held depressed.

    (iii) The hood may be jettisoned in emergency (see para. 59).

32. **Signal discharger.**—The recognition device fires one of six cartridges out of the top of the rear fuselage when the handle (39) to the left of the pilot's seat is pulled upwards. On some aircraft a pre-selector control (38) is mounted above the operating handle.

PART II

HANDLING

33. **Management of the fuel system**

NOTE.—Except for special operations as directed by the appropriate Area Commander, the rear fuselage tanks must not be used and their cocks should be wired OFF. On aircraft with " rear view " fuselages they must not be used.

(i) *Without a drop tank*

Start the engine, warm up, taxy and take-off on the main tanks; then, at 2,000 ft., change to the rear fuselage tanks (turning off the main tanks cock after the change has been made) and drain them; then revert to the main tanks.

(ii) *When fitted with a drop tank*

(*a*) *Without rear fuselage tanks:* Start the engine, warm up, taxy and take-off on the main tanks; then at 2,000 ft. turn ON the drop tank and turn OFF the main tanks cock. When the fuel pressure warning light comes on, or the engine cuts, turn OFF the drop tank cock and reselect the main tanks. (See Note (i) below.)

(*b*) *With rear fuselage tanks:* Start the engine, warm up, taxy and take-off on the main tanks; then, at 2,000 ft. change to the rear fuselage tanks and continue to use fuel from them until they contain only 30 gallons. Turn ON the drop tank (turning OFF the rear fuselage tanks cock when the change has been made) and drain it, then change back to the rear fuselage tanks and drain them. Revert to the main tanks.

NOTE.— (i) When it is essential to use all the fuel from the drop tank its cock must be turned OFF and the throttle closed immediately the engine cuts; a fresh tank should then be selected

PART II—HANDLING

without delay. The booster pump in the newly selected tank should be switched ON, or the hand wobble pump operated, to assist the engine to pick up but in addition to this it may be necessary to windmill the engine at high r.p.m. to ensure an adequate fuel supply.

(ii) Drop tanks should only be jettisoned if this is necessary operationally. If a drop tank is jettisoned before it is empty a fresh tank should be turned ON before the drop tank cock is turned OFF.

(iii) At no time must the drop tank cock and the rear fuselage tanks cock be on together or fuel from the rear fuselage tanks will drain into the drop tank since the connection from these tanks joins the drop tank connection below the non-return valve.

(iv) The drop tank cock must always be off when the tank has been jettisoned or is empty, otherwise air may be drawn into the main fuel system thus causing engine cutting.

(iii) *Use of the booster pump(s)*

(*a*) The main tanks booster pump should be switched ON for take-off and landing and at all times when these tanks are in use in flight.

(*b*) The rear fuselage tanks booster pump should be switched ON at all times when changing to, or using fuel from, these tanks.

34. Preliminaries

(i) Check that the undercarriage selector lever is down; switch on indicator and see that DOWN shows green.

(ii) Check the contents of the fuel tanks. If fitted with auxiliary tank(s) check that corresponding cock(s) are OFF.

(iii) Test the operation of the flying controls and adjust the rudder pedals for equal length.

PART II—HANDLING

(iv) On aircraft with Bendix-Stromberg carburettors ensure that the idle cut-off control is in the fully aft position, or cut-off position (see para. 25), then check the operation of the booster pump(s) by sound.

35. **Starting the engine and warming up** (Aircraft with Merlin 61 or 63 engines)

(i) Set the fuel cock .. .. ON

(ii) Ignition switches .. .. OFF
Throttle .. .. .. $\frac{1}{2}$ in. – 1 in. open
Propeller speed control lever Fully forward
Supercharger switch .. AUTO. NORMAL POSITION
Carburettor air intake filter control CLOSED or FILTER IN OPERATION (see para. 26)

(iii) If an external priming connection is fitted, high volatility fuel (Stores ref. 34A/III) should be used for priming at temperatures below freezing. Work the Ki-gass priming pump until the fuel reaches the priming nozzles; this may be judged by a sudden increase in resistance.

(iv) Switch ON the ignition and press the starter and booster-coil buttons. Turning periods must not exceed 20 seconds, with a 30 seconds wait between each. Work the priming pump as rapidly and vigorously as possible while the engine is being turned; it should start after the following number of strokes if cold:

Air temperature °C.	+30	+20	+10	0	−10	−20
Normal fuel	3	4	7	12	—	—
High volatility fuel	—	—	—	4	8	18

(v) At temperatures below freezing it will probably be necessary to continue priming after the engine has fired and until it picks up on the carburettor.

(vi) Release the starter button as soon as the engine starts, and as soon as the engine is running satisfactorily release the booster-coil button and screw down the priming pump.

(vii) Open up slowly to 1,000 to 1,200 r.p.m., then warm up at this speed.

PART II—HANDLING

36. **Starting the engine and warming up** (Aircraft with Merlin 66, 70 or 266 engines)

   (i) Set the fuel cock   ON

   (ii) Ignition switches .. .. OFF
   Throttle .. .. .. $\frac{1}{2}$ in. – 1 in. open
   Propeller speed control (or override) lever .. .. Fully forward
   Idle cut-off control .. .. Fully aft
   Supercharger switch .. AUTO. NORMAL POSITION
   Carburettor air intake filter control   CLOSED or FILTER IN OPERATION (see para. 26)

   (iii) Switch ON the main tanks booster pump for 30 seconds (or operate the hand wobble pump for that period) then switch it OFF and set the idle cut-off control forward to the RUN position.

   > NOTE.—If the idle cut-off control is operated by the ring described in para. 25, this must be held out (i.e., in the cut-off position) while the booster pump is ON or the hand wobble pump is being used.

   (iv) An external priming connection is fitted and high volatility fuel (Stores Ref. 34A/111) should be used for priming at temperatures below freezing. Operate the priming pump until fuel reaches the priming nozzles (this may be judged by a sudden increase in resistance to the plunger) then prime the engine (if it is cold) with the following number of strokes

Air temperature °C.	+30	+20	+10	0	−10	−20
Normal fuel	3	4	7	12	—	—
High volatility fuel	—	—	—	4	8	18

   (v) Switch ON the ignition and press the starter and booster-coil pushbuttons.

   (vi) When the engine fires release the starter button; keep the booster-coil button depressed and operate the priming pump (if required) until the engine is running smoothly.

PART II—HANDLING

(vii) Screw down the priming pump then open up gradually to 1,000–1,200 r.p.m. and warm up at this speed.

(viii) Check that the fuel pressure warning light does not come on then switch ON the main tanks booster pump (if fitted).

37. Testing the engine and services while warming up

(i) Check all temperatures and pressures and the operation of the flaps.

(ii) Press the radiator flaps test pushbutton and have the ground crew check that the flaps open.

(iii) Test each magneto in turn as a precautionary check before increasing power further.

(iv) If a drop tank is carried check the flow of fuel from it by running on it for at least one minute.

After warming up to at least 15° C. (oil temperature) and 60° C. (coolant temperature),

(v) Open up to 0 lb./sq.in. boost and exercise and check the operation of the two-speed two-stage supercharger by pressing in and holding the test pushbutton. Boost should rise slightly and the red warning light should come on when high gear is engaged. Release the pushbutton after 30 seconds.

(vi) At the same boost, exercise (at least twice) and check the operation of the constant speed propeller by moving the speed control lever over its full governing range. Return the lever fully forward. Check that the generator is charging the accumulator by noting that the power failure warning light is out.

(vii) Test each magneto in turn; if the single ignition drop exceeds 150 r.p.m., the ignition should be checked at higher power—see sub. para. (ix) below.

> NOTE.—*The following additional checks should be carried out after repair, inspection other than daily, when the single ignition drop at 0 lb./sq.in. boost exceeds 150 r.p.m., or at any time at the discretion of the pilot. When these checks are performed the tail of the aircraft must be securely lashed down.*

PART II—HANDLING

(viii) Open the throttle to the take-off setting and check boost and static r.p.m.

(ix) Throttle back until r.p.m. fall just below the take-off figure (thus ensuring that the propeller is not constant speeding) then test each magneto in turn. If the single ignition drop exceeds 150 r.p.m. the aircraft should not be flown.

(x) Where applicable (see para. 20) throttle back to +3 lb./sq.in. boost and set the override lever to AUTOMATIC; r.p.m. should fall to 1,800–1,850. Return the lever to MAX. R.P.M.

(xi) Before taxying check the brake pressure (80 lb./sq.in.) and the pneumatic supply pressure (220 lb./sq.in.).

38. Check list before take-off

T—Trimming tabs

	At training load (full main tanks, no ammunition or external stores) 7,150 lb. (All Marks)	At normal full load (full main tanks, ammunition + 1 x 45-gallon "blister" drop tank) 7,800 lb. (Max. Mk. XI)	At max. load (full main and rear fuselage tanks, full ammunition, + 1 x 90-gallon "blister" drop tank) 8,700 lb. (IX & XVI)
Elevator	1 div. nose down	Neutral	1 div. nose down
Rudder	Fully right	Fully right	Fully right

P—Propeller control   Speed control (or override) lever fully forward

F—Fuel   Main tanks cock—ON
Drop tank cock—OFF
Rear fuselage tanks cock—OFF
Main tanks booster pump—ON

F—Flaps   UP

Supercharger   Switch—AUTO-NORMAL POSITION
Red light out

Carburettor air intake filter control   CLOSED or FILTER IN OPERATION (see para. 26)

PART II—HANDLING

39. Take-off

(i) At training and normal loads +7 lb./sq.in. to +9 lb./sq. in. boost is sufficient for take-off. After take-off, however, boost should be increased (where applicable) to +12lb./sq.in. to minimise the possibility of lead fouling of the sparking plugs.

(ii) There is a tendency to swing to the left but this can easily be checked with the rudder.

(iii) When the rear fuselage tanks are full the aircraft pitches on becoming airborne and it is recommended that the undercarriage should not be retracted, nor the sliding hood closed, until a height of at least 100 feet has been reached.

(iv) After retracting the undercarriage it is essential to check that the red warning light comes on, since if the undercarriage fails to lock UP the airflow through the radiators and oil cooler will be much reduced and excessive temperatures will result.

> NOTE.—It may be necessary to hold the undercarriage selector lever hard forward against the quadrant until the red warning light comes on.

(v) If interconnected throttle and propeller controls are fitted move the override lever smoothly back to AUTOMATIC when comfortably airborne.

(vi) After take-off some directional retrimming will be necessary.

(vii) Unless operating in sandy or dust-laden conditions set the carburettor air intake filter control to OPEN (or NORMAL INTAKE) at 1,000 ft.

40. Climbing

At all loads the recommended climbing speed is 180 m.p.h. (155 kts) I.A.S. from sea level to operating height.

> NOTE.— (i) With the supercharger switch at AUTO, high gear is engaged automatically when the aircraft reaches a predetermined height (see para. 21). This is the optimum height for the gear change if full combat power is being

used, but if normal climbing power (2,850 r.p.m. + 12 lb./sq.in. boost) is being used the maximum rate of climb is obtained by delaying the gear change until the boost in low gear has fallen to + 8 lb./sq.in.

This is achieved by leaving the supercharger switch at MS until the boost has fallen to this figure.

(ii) Use of the air intake filter reduces the full throttle height considerably.

41. General flying

(i) *Stability*

(*a*) At light load (no fuel in the rear fuselage tanks, no drop tank) stability about all axes is satisfactory and the aircraft is easy and pleasant to fly.

(*b*) When the rear fuselage tanks are full there is a very marked reduction in longitudinal stability, the aircraft tightens in turns at all altitudes and, in this condition, is restricted to straight flying, and only gentle manœuvres; accurate trimming is not possible and instrument flying should be avoided whenever possible.

(*c*) When a 90-gallon drop tank is carried in addition to full fuel in the rear fuselage tanks the aircraft becomes extremely difficult and tiring to fly and in this condition is restricted to straight flying and only gentle manœuvres at low altitudes.

(*d*) On aircraft which have " rear view " fuselages there is a reduction in directional stability so that the application of yaw promotes marked changes of lateral and longitudinal trim. This characteristic is more pronounced at high altitudes.

(*e*) When 90 (or 170) gallon drop tanks are carried on these aircraft, they are restricted to straight flying and gentle manœuvres only.

(ii) *Controls*

The elevator and rudder trimming tabs are powerful and sensitive and must always be used with care, particularly at high speed.

PART II—HANDLING

(iii) *Changes of trim*

Undercarriage up	Nose up
Undercarriage down	Nose down
Flaps up	Nose up
Flaps down	Strongly nose down

There are marked changes of directional trim with change of power and speed. These should be countered by accurate use of the rudder trimming tab control.

The firing of salvos of R/P's promotes a nose-up change of trim; this change of trim is most marked when the weapons are fired in level flight at about 300 m.p.h. (258 kts) I.A.S.

(iv) *Flying at reduced airspeed in conditions of poor visibility.* Reduce speed to 160 m.p.h. (140 kts) I.A.S., lower the flaps and set the propeller speed control (or override) lever to give 2,650 r.p.m.; open the sliding hood. Speed may then be reduced to 140 m.p.h. (120 kts) I.A.S.

42. Stalling

(i) The stalling speeds, engine "off", in m.p.h. (knots) I.A.S. are

Aircraft without "rear-view" fuselages

	At training load (full main tanks, no ammunition or external stores) 7,150 lb.	At normal full load (full main tanks, full ammunition + 1 × 45-gallon "blister" drop tank) 7,800 lb.	At maximum load (full main and rear fuselage tanks, full ammunition + 1 × 90-gallon "blister" drop tank) 8,700 lb.
Undercarriage and flaps up	90 (78)	93 (80)	100 (86)
Undercarriage and flaps down	75–79 (65–69)	80 (69)	84 (72)

Aircraft with "rear view" fuselages

Undercarriage and flaps up	95 (83)	98 (85)	115–117 (100–102)
Undercarriage and flaps down	82–84 (71–73)	85 (98)	95 (83)

The speeds above apply to aircraft which have "clipped" wings. On aircraft with "full span" wings these speeds are reduced (at all loads by some 3–6 m.p.h. (or kts) I.A.S.

PART II—HANDLING

(ii) Warning of the approach of a stall is given by tail buffeting, the onset of which can be felt some 10 m.p.h. (9 kts) I.A.S. before the stall itself. At the stall either wing and the nose drop gently. Recovery is straightforward and easy.

If the control column is held back at the stall tail buffeting becomes very pronounced and the wing drop is more marked.

> NOTE.—On L.F. Mk. XVI aircraft warning of the approach of a stall is not so clear; faint tail buffeting can be felt some 5 m.p.h. (or kts) I.A.S. before the stall occurs.

(iii) When the rear fuselage tanks are full there is an increasing tendency for the nose to rise as the stall is approached. This self-stalling tendency must be checked by firm forward movement of the control column.

(iv) Warning of the approach of a stall in a steep turn is given by pronounced tail buffeting (and on F. Mk. XVI aircraft by hood rattling). If the acceleration is then increased the aircraft will, in general, flick out of the turn.

43. Spinning

(i) Spinning is permitted, but the loss of height involved in recovery may be very great and the following limits are to be observed:

(a) Spins are not to be started below 10,000 feet.

(b) Recovery must be initiated before two turns are completed.

(ii) A speed of 180 m.p.h. (156 kts) I.A.S. should be attained before starting to ease out of the resultant dive.

(iii) Spinning is not permitted when fitted with a drop tank, when carrying a bomb load, or with any fuel in the rear fuselage tank.

44. Diving

(i) At training loads the aircraft becomes increasingly tail heavy as speed is gained and should, therefore, be trimmed into the dive. The tendency to yaw to the right should be corrected by accurate use of the rudder trimming tab control.

PART II—HANDLING

(ii) When carrying wing bombs the angle of dive must not exceed 60°; when carrying a fuselage bomb the angle of dive must not exceed 40°.

> NOTE.—Until the rear fuselage tanks contain less than 30 gallons of fuel the aircraft is restricted to straight flight and only gentle manœuvres.

45. Aerobatics

(i) Aerobatics are not permitted when carrying any external stores (except the 30-gallon " blister " drop tank) nor when the rear fuselage tanks contain more than 30 gallons of fuel, *and are not recommended when the rear fuselage tanks contain any fuel*.

(ii) The following minimum speeds in m.p.h. (knots) I.A.S. are recommended:

Loop	300 (260)
Roll	240 (206)
Half-roll off loop	340 (295)
Climbing roll	330 (286)

(iii) Flick manoeuvres are not permitted.

46. Check list before landing

(i) Reduce speed to 160 m.p.h. (138 kts) I.A.S., open the sliding hood and check:

U—Undercarriage	DOWN
P—Propeller control	Speed control (or override) lever set to give 2,650 r.p.m.—fully forward on the final approach
Supercharger	Red light out
Carburettor air intake filter control	CLOSED (or FILTER IN OPERATION)—see para. 26.
F—Fuel	Main tanks cock ON. Main tanks booster pump (if fitted)—ON
F—Flaps	DOWN

(ii) Check brake pressure (80 lb./sq.in.) and pneumatic supply pressure (220 lb./sq.in.).

> NOTE.—The rate of undercarriage lowering is much reduced at low r.p.m.

PART II—HANDLING

47. Approach and landing

(i) The recommended final approach speeds* in m.p.h. (kts) I.A.S. are

At training load (full main tanks, no ammunition or external stores) 7,150 lb.

(a) Aircraft without "rear-view" fuselages

	Engine assisted	Glide
Flaps down	95 (82)	105 (90)
Flaps up	105 (90)	110 (95)

(b) Aircraft with "rear-view" fuselages

	Engine assisted	Glide
Flaps down	100–105 (86–90)	115–120 (100–104)
Flaps up	115 (100)	120–125 (104–108)

*These are the speeds at which the airfield boundary is crossed; the initial straight approach should, however, be made at a speed 20–25 m.p.h. (17–21 kts) I.A.S. above these figures.

NOTE.—The speeds above apply to aircraft which have "clipped" wings; on aircraft with "full span" wings they may be safely reduced by 5 m.p.h. (or kts) I.A.S.

(ii) Should it be necessary in emergency to land with the rear fuselage tanks still containing all their fuel the final engine-assisted approach speeds given in (i) above should be increased by 10–15 m.p.h. (9–13 kts) I.A.S. The tendency for the nose to rise of its own accord at the "hold-off" must be watched (see para. 42 (iii)); the throttle should be closed only when contact with the ground is made.

(iii) The aircraft is nose-heavy on the ground; the brakes, therefore, must be used carefully on landing.

48. Mislanding

(i) At normal loads the aircraft will climb away easily with the undercarriage and flaps down and the use of full take-off power is unnecessary.

PART II—HANDLING

(ii) Open the throttle steadily to give the required boost.
(iii) Retract the undercarriage immediately.
(iv) With the flaps down climb at about 140 m.p.h. I.A.S.
(v) Raise the flaps at 300 ft. and retrim.

49. Beam approach

SPITFIRE Mk. XVI, at "training" load	Preliminary Approach	Inner Marker on Q.D.R.	Outer Marker on Q.D.R.	Inner Marker on Q.D.M.
Indicated height (ft.)	Down to 1,000	1,000	700–800	150
Action	—	Lower the undercarriage†	Lower the flaps	Throttle back slowly
Resultant change of trim	—	Nose down	Nose down	Slightly nose down
I.A.S. m.p.h. (knots)	170 (146)	160 (138)	130 (112)	110 (95)
R.P.M.	2,650	2,650	3,000*	3,000*
Boost (level flight)	−2	−2	−3	
Boost (−500 ft./min.)	−3	−3	−4	
Boost (overshoot)	—	—	—	+7

Remarks
† Reduce speed to 160 m.p.h. (138 kts) I.A.S. before lowering the undercarriage.
* With the override lever at MAX. R.P.M., r.p.m. may be 3,000–3,050 (see para. 20)
Altimeter error at take-off −50 ft.
Altimeter error at touchdown −60 ft.
Add 2 mbs. to Q.F.E. to give zero reading at touchdown.

OVERSHOOT
Open the throttle to give +7 lb./sq.in. boost.
Raise the undercarriage and climb at 130 m.p.h. (112 kts) I.A.S.
Raise the flaps at 300 ft. and retrim.

PART II—HANDLING

50. After landing

(i) *Before taxying*

Raise the flaps and switch OFF the main tanks booster pump (if fitted).

(ii) *On reaching dispersal*

(*a*) Open up to 0 lb./sq.in. boost and exercise the two-speed two-stage supercharger once (see para. 35 (v)).

(*b*) Throttle back slowly to 800–900 r.p.m. and idle at this speed for a few seconds then stop the engine by operating the slow running cut-out or idle cut-off control.

(*c*) When the propeller has stopped rotating switch OFF the ignition and all other electrical services.

(*d*) Turn OFF the fuel.

(iii) *Oil dilution (see A.P. 2095)*

The correct dilution periods are

At air temperatures above $-10°$ C. .. 1 minute.
At air temperatures below $-10°$ C. .. 2 minutes.

AIR PUBLICATION 1565J, P & L—P.N.
Pilot's Notes

PART III

OPERATING DATA

51. **Engine data : Merlins 61, 63, 66, 70 and 266**

(i) Fuel—100 octane only.

(ii) Oil—See A.P. 1464/C.37.

(iii) The principal engine limitations are as follows :

	Sup.	R.p.m.	Boost	Temp. °C. Coolant	Oil
MAX. TAKE-OFF TO 1,000 FT.	M	3,000†	+18*	135	—
MAX. CLIMBING 1 HOUR LIMIT	M S	2,850	+12	125	90
MAXIMUM CONTINUOUS	M S	2,650	+ 7	105 (115)	90
COMBAT 5 MINS. LIMIT	M S	3,000	+18‡	135	105

The figure in brackets is permissible for short periods.

† With interconnected controls there is a tolerance on "maximum" r.p.m.—see para. 20.

* +12 lb./sq.in. on Merlin 61 and 63 engines.

‡ +15 lb./sq.in. on Merlin 61 engine.

OIL PRESSURE:
   MINIMUM IN FLIGHT .. .. .. 30 lb./sq.in.

MINIMUM TEMP. °C. FOR TAKE-OFF:
   COOLANT .. .. 60° C.
   OIL .. .. 15° C.

PART III—OPERATING DATA

52. Flying limitations

(i) *Maximum speeds in m.p.h. (knots) I.A.S.*

Diving (without external stores), corresponding to a Mach. No. of ·85:

Between S.L. and 20,000 ft.—450 (385)
20,000 & 25,000 ft.—430 (370)
25,000 & 30,000 ft.—390 (335)
30,000 & 35,000 ft.—340 (292)
Above 35,000 ft.—310 (265)
Undercarriage down —160 (138)
Flaps down —160 (138)

Diving (with the following external stores):

(a) With 1 × 500 lb. AN/M 58 bomb,
or 1 × 500 lb. AN/M 64 bomb,
or 1 × 500 lb. AN/M 76 bomb,
or 1 × 65 nickel bomb Mk. II
Below 20,000 ft.*—440 (378)

(b) With 1 × 500 lb. S.A.P. bomb
or Smoke bomb Mk. II
Below 25,000 ft.*—400 (344)

(c) With 10 lb. practice bomb
Below 25,000 ft.*—420 (360)

*Above these heights the limitations for the " clean " aircraft apply.

(ii) *Maximum weights in lbs.*

For take-off and gentle
manœuvres only .. .. Mks. IX & XVI—8,700*
For landing (except in
emergency) .. .. Mks. IX & XVI—7,450
For take-off, all forms of
flying and landing .. Mk. XI —7,800

*At this weight take-off must be made only from a smooth hard runway.

(iii) *Flying restrictions*

(a) Rear fuselage tanks may be used only with special authority and never on aircraft with " rear view " fuselages.

PART III—OPERATING DATA

(*b*) Aerobatics and combat manœuvres are not permitted when carrying any external stores (except the 30-gallon " blister " type drop tank) nor when the rear fuselage tanks contain more than 30 gallons of fuel (but see para. 45).

(*c*) When a 90 (or 170) gallon drop tank or a bomb load is carried the aircraft is restricted to straight flying and only gentle manœuvres.

(*d*) When wing bombs are carried in addition to a drop tank or fuselage bomb, take-off must be made only from a smooth hard runway.

(*e*) When carried, the 90 (or 170) gallon drop tank must be jettisoned before any dive bombing is commenced.

(*f*) The angle of dive when releasing a bomb or bomb load must not exceed 60° for wing bombs or 40° for a fuselage bomb.

(*g*) Except in emergency the fuselage bomb or drop tank must be jettisoned before landing with wing bombs fitted.

(*h*) Drop tanks should not be jettisoned unless necessary operationally. While jettisoning, the aircraft should be flown straight and level at a speed not greater than 300 m.p.h. I.A.S.

(*i*) Except in emergency landings should not be attempted until the rear fuselage tanks contain less than 30 gallons of fuel. Should a landing be necessary when they contain a greater quantity of fuel the drop tank (if fitted) should be jettisoned.

53. Position error corrections

From To	120 150	150 170	170 210	210 240	240 290	290 350	m.p.h. I.A.S.
Add Subtract	4	2	0 0	2	4	6	m.p.h. or kts.
From To	106 130	130 147	147 180	180 208	208 250	250 300	Knots I.A.S.

PART III—OPERATING DATA

54. Maximum performance

(i) *Climbing*

(*a*) The speeds in m.p.h. (knots) for maximum rate of climb are

Sea level to 26,000 ft.—160 (140) I.A.S.
26,000 ft. to 30,000 ft.—150 (130) ,,
30,000 ft. to 33,000 ft.—140 (122) ,,
33,000 ft. to 37,000 ft.—130 (112) ,,
37,000 ft. to 40,000 ft.—120 (104) ,,
Above 40,000 ft.   —110 (95) ,,

(*b*) With the supercharger switch at AUTO, high gear is engaged automatically when the aircraft reaches a predetermined height (see para. 21). This is the optimum height for the gear change if full combat power is being used, but if normal climbing power (2,850 r.p.m. + 12 lb./sq.in. boost) is being used the maximum rate of climb is obtained by delaying the gear change until the boost in low gear has fallen to +8 lb./sq.in.

This is achieved by leaving the supercharger switch at MS until the boost has fallen to this figure.

(ii) *Combat*

Set the supercharger switch to AUTO and open the throttle fully.

> NOTE.—On those aircraft which do not have interconnected throttle and propeller controls the propeller speed control lever must be advanced to the maximum r.p.m. position before the throttle is opened fully.

55. Economical flying

(i) *Climbing*

On aircraft not fitted with interconnected throttle and propeller controls.

(*a*) Set the supercharger switch to MS, the propeller speed control lever to give 2,650 r.p.m. and climb at the

PART III—OPERATING DATA

speeds given in para. 54 (i), opening the throttle progressively to maintain a boost pressure of $+7$ lb./sq.in.

(b) Set the supercharger switch to AUTO when the maximum obtainable boost in low gear is $+3$ lb./sq.in., throttling back to prevent overboosting as the change to high gear is made.

On aircraft fitted with interconnected throttle and propeller controls

(a) Set the supercharger switch to MS, set the throttle to give $+7$ lb./sq.in. boost and climb at the speeds given in para. 54 (i).

(b) As height is gained the boost will fall and it will be necessary to advance the throttle progressively to restore it. The throttle must not, however, be advanced beyond a position at which r.p.m. rise to 2,650. Set the supercharger switch to AUTO when, at this throttle setting, the boost in low gear has fallen to $+3$ lb./sq.in.

NOTE.—Climbing at the speeds given in para. 54 (i) will ensure greatest range, but for ease of control (especially at heavy loads and with the rear fuselage tanks full of fuel) a climbing speed of 180 m.p.h. (155 kts) I.A.S. from sea level to operating height is recommended. The loss of range will be only slight.

(ii) *Cruising*

The recommended speed for maximum range is 170 m.p.h. (147 kts) I.A.S. if the aircraft is lightly loaded. At heavy loads, especially if the rear fuselage tanks are full this speed can be increased to 200 m.p.h. (172 kts) I.A.S. without incurring a serious loss of range.

PART III—OPERATING DATA

On aircraft not fitted with interconnected throttle and propeller controls

(a) With the supercharger switch at MS fly at the maximum obtainable boost (not exceeding + 7 lb./sq.in.) and obtain the recommended speed by reducing r.p.m. as required.

NOTE.— (i) R.p.m. should not be reduced below a minimum of 1,800. At low altitudes, therefore, it may be necessary to reduce boost or the recommended speed will be exceeded.

(ii) As the boost falls at high altitudes it will not be possible to maintain the recommended speed in low gear, even at maximum continuous r.p.m. and full throttle. It will then be necessary to set the supercharger switch to AUTO. Boost will thus be restored and it will be possible to reduce r.p.m. again (as outlined in (a) above).

(iii) In both low and high gears r.p.m. which promote rough running should be avoided.

On aircraft fitted with interconnected throttle and propeller controls

Set the supercharger switch to MS and adjust the throttle to obtain the recommended speed. Avoid a throttle setting which promotes rough running.

NOTE.—At moderate and high altitudes it will be necessary to advance the throttle progressively to restore the falling boost and thus maintain the recommended speed.

Now as the throttle is opened r.p.m. will increase and at a certain height the recommended speed will be unobtainable even at a throttle setting which gives 2,650 r.p.m. At this height the supercharger switch should be set to AUTO and the throttle then adjusted as before to maintain the recommended speed.

PART III—OPERATING DATA

56. Fuel capacities and consumption

(i) *Normal fuel capacity:*

Top tank	48 gallons
Bottom tank	37 gallons
Total	85 gallons

(ii) *Long-range fuel capacities:*

With 30-gallon " blister " drop tank	115 gallons
With 45-gallon " blister " drop tank	130 gallons
With 90-gallon " blister " drop tank	175 gallons
With 170-gallon " blister " drop tank	255 gallons
With rear fuselage tanks	
Early aircraft	160 gallons
Later aircraft	151 gallons

NOTE.—On some aircraft these capacities are increased by 10 gallons.

(iii) *Fuel consumptions:*

The approximate fuel consumptions (gals./hr.) are as follows:

Weak mixture (as obtained at $+7$ lb./sq.in. boost and below):

Boost lb./sq.in.	R.p.m.				
	2,650	2,400	2,200	2,000	1,800
+7	80	—	—	—	—
+4	71	66	61	54	—
+2	66	61	57	50	43
0	60	55	51	45	39
−2	53	49	45	40	35
−4	45	42	38	34	30

PART III—OPERATING DATA

Rich mixture (as obtained above $+ 7$ lb./sq.in. boost):

Boost lb./sq.in.	R.p.m.	gals./hr.
$+15$	3,000	130
$+12$	2,850	105

NOTE.—The above approximate consumptions apply for all Marks of engine. Accurate figures giving the variation in consumption with height and as between low and high gear are not available.

PART IV

EMERGENCIES

57. Undercarriage emergency operation

(i) If the selector lever jams and cannot be moved to the fully down position after moving it out of the gate, return it to the fully forward position for a few seconds to take the weight of the wheels off the locking pins and allow them to turn freely, then move it to the DOWN position.

(ii) If, however, the lever is jammed so that it cannot be moved either forward or downward, it can be released by taking the weight of the wheels off the locking pins either by pushing the control column forward sharply or inverting the aircraft. The lever can then be moved to the DOWN position.

(iii) If the lever springs into the gate and the indicator shows that the undercarriage is not locked down, hold it fully down for a few seconds. If this is not successful, raise and then lower the undercarriage again.

(iv) If the undercarriage still does not lock down, ensure that the lever is in the DOWN position (this is essential) and push the emergency lever forward and downward through 180°.

> NOTE.—(*a*) The emergency lever must not be returned to its original position and no attempt must be made to raise the undercarriage until the CO_2 cylinder has been replaced.
>
> (*b*) If the CO_2 cylinder has been accidentally discharged with the selector lever in the up position, the undercarriage will not lower unless the pipeline from the cylinder is broken, either by hand or by means of the crowbar.

PART IV—EMERGENCIES

58. Failure of the pneumatic system

(i) If the flaps fail to lower when the control is moved to the DOWN position, it is probably due to a leak in the pipeline, resulting in complete loss of air pressure and consequent brake failure.

(ii) Alternatively, if a leak develops in the flaps control system the flaps will lower, but complete loss of air pressure will follow and the brakes will become inoperative. (In this case a hissing sound may be heard in the cockpit after selecting flaps DOWN.)

(iii) In either case the flaps control should immediately be returned to the UP position in order to allow sufficient pressure to build up, so that a landing can be made with the brakes operative but without flaps.

> NOTE.—As a safeguard pilots should always check the pneumatic pressure supply after selecting flaps DOWN.

59. Hood jettisoning

The hood may be jettisoned in an emergency by pulling the rubber knob inside the top of the hood forward and downward and then pushing the lower edge of the hood outwards with the elbows.

> WARNING.—Before jettisoning the hood the seat should be lowered and the head then kept well down.

60. Forced landing

In the event of engine failure necessitating a forced landing:

(i) If a drop tank or bomb load is carried it should be jettisoned.

(ii) The fuel cut-off control (if fitted) should be pulled fully back.

(iii) The booster pump (if fitted) should be switched OFF.

PART IV—EMERGENCIES

(iv) The sliding hood should be opened and the cockpit door set on the catch (see para. 31).

(v) A speed of at least 150 m.p.h. (130 kts) I.A.S. should be maintained while manœuvring with the undercarriage and flaps retracted.

(vi) The flaps must not be lowered until it is certain that the selected landing area is within easy gliding reach.

(vii) The final straight approach should be made at the speeds given in para. 47.

(viii) If oil pressure is still available the glide can be lengthened considerably by pulling the propeller speed control (or override) lever fully back past the stop in the quadrant.

61. Ditching

(i) Whenever possible the aircraft should be abandoned by parachute rather than ditched, since the ditching qualities are known to be very poor.

(ii) When ditching is inevitable any external stores should be jettisoned (release will be more certain if the aircraft is gliding straight) and the following procedure observed:

(*a*) The cockpit hood should be jettisoned.

(*b*) The flaps should be lowered in order to reduce the touchdown speed as much as possible.

(*c*) The undercarriage should be kept retracted.

(*d*) The safety harness should be kept tightly adjusted and the R/T plug should be disconnected.

(*e*) The engine, if available, should be used to help make the touchdown in a taildown attitude at as low a forward speed as possible.

PART IV—EMERGENCIES

(*f*) Ditching should be along the swell, or into wind if the swell is not steep, but the pilot should be prepared for a tendency for the aircraft to dive when contact with the water is made.

62. **Crowbar**

A crowbar for use in emergency is stowed in spring clips on the cockpit door.

PART V—*ILLUSTRATIONS*

KEY to Figs. 1, 2 and 3

1. Ignition switches.
2. Undercarriage indicator.
3. Oxygen regulator.
4. Navigation lamps switch.
5. Flap control.
6. Instrument flying panel.
7. Lifting ring for sunscreen.
8. Reflector sight switch.
9. Reflector sight base.
10. Voltmeter.
11. Cockpit ventilator control.
12. Engine-speed indicator.
13. Supercharger warning lamp.
14. Boost gauge.
15. Intercooler protector pushbutton.
16. Coolant temperature gauge.
17. Oil temperature gauge.
18. Fuel pressure warning lamp.
19. Fuel contents gauge and pushbutton.
20. Oil pressure gauge.
21. Engine starter pushbutton.
22. Booster-coil pushbutton.
23. Cockpit floodlight switches.
24. Elevator tab position indicator.
25. Brake triple pressure gauge.
26. Crowbar.
27. Rudder trimming tab handwheel.
28. Pressure-head heater switch.
29. Two-position door catch lever.
30. Elevator trimming tab handwheel.
31. Throttle lever friction adjuster.
32. Floodlight.
33. Throttle lever.
34. Undercarriage indicator master switch.
35. Propeller speed control.
36. T.R.1133 pushbutton control.
37. Slow-running cut-out.
38. Signal discharger pre-selector control.
39. Signal discharger firing control.
40. Power failure lamp.
41. Radiator ground test pushbutton.
42. Supercharger ground test pushbutton.
43. Oil dilution pushbutton.
44. Map case.
45. Rudder pedal adjusting starwheel.
46. Propeller control friction adjuster.
47. Fuel cock control.
48. Engine priming pump.
49. Signalling switchbox.
50. Fuel tank pressure cock.
51. Remote contactor and contactor switch.
52. Undercarriage control lever.
53. IFF pushbuttons.
54. Harness release control.
55. IFF master switch.
56. Undercarriage emergency lowering control.
57. Rudder pedal adjusting starwheel.
58. Drop tank cock control.
59. Drop tank jettison lever.
60. Windscreen de-icing cock.
61. Seat adjustment lever.
62. Windscreen de-icing needle valve.
63. Windscreen de-icing pump.
64. Microphone/telephone socket.
65. Oxygen supply cock.

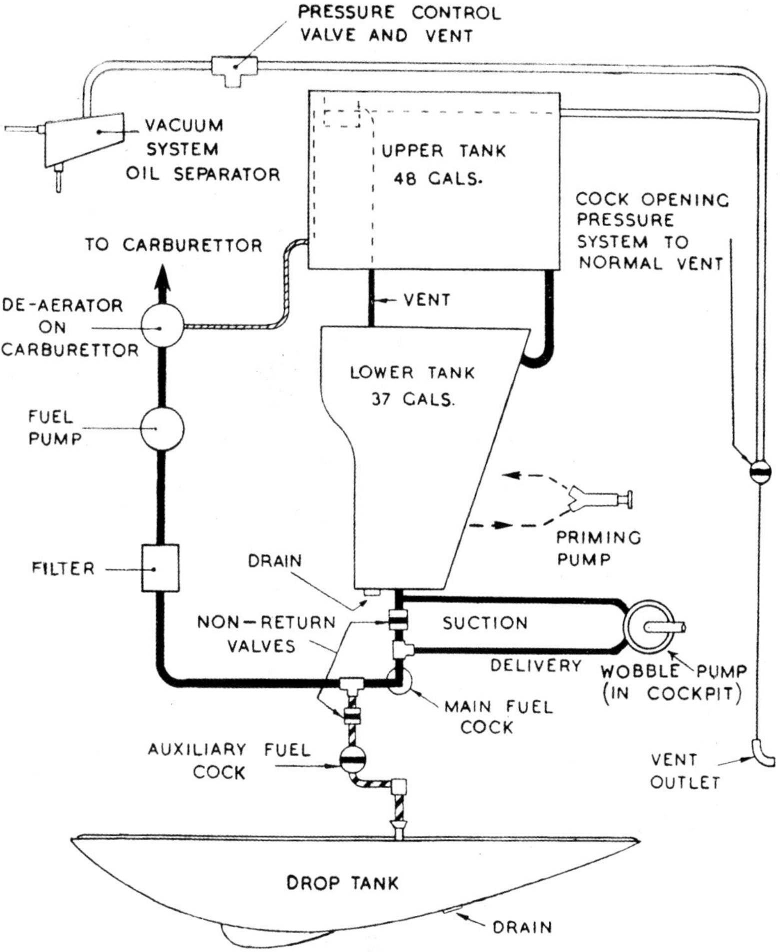

WOBBLE PUMP INSTALLATION
EARLY MERLIN 66 & 70 ENGINES

MAIN FUEL SYSTEM	▬▬▬▬	DE-AERATOR SYSTEM	▬ ▬ ▬
AUXILIARY SYSTEM	▰▰▰▰	PRESSURE SYSTEM	═══
PRIMING SYSTEM	– – ▸ – –	WOBBLE PUMP SYSTEM	▬▬▬▬

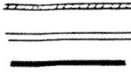

M DIAGRAM
TED WITH BOOSTER OR WOBBLE PUMPS

FIG 4

FIG. 1

INSTRUME

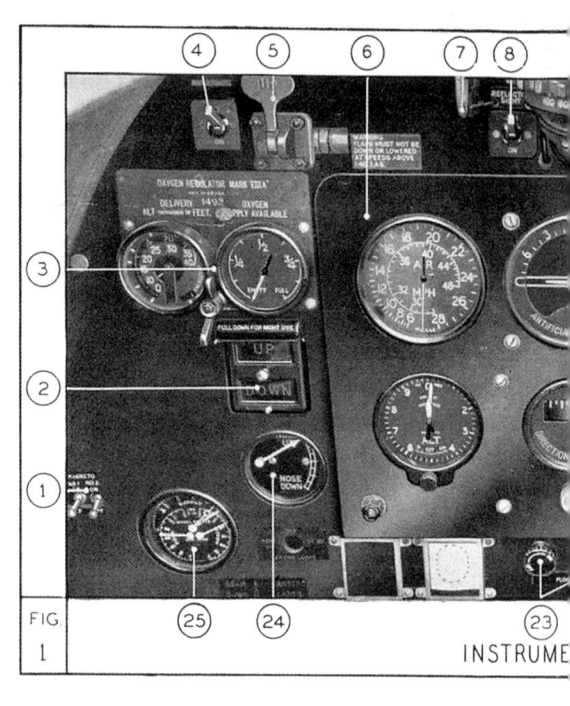

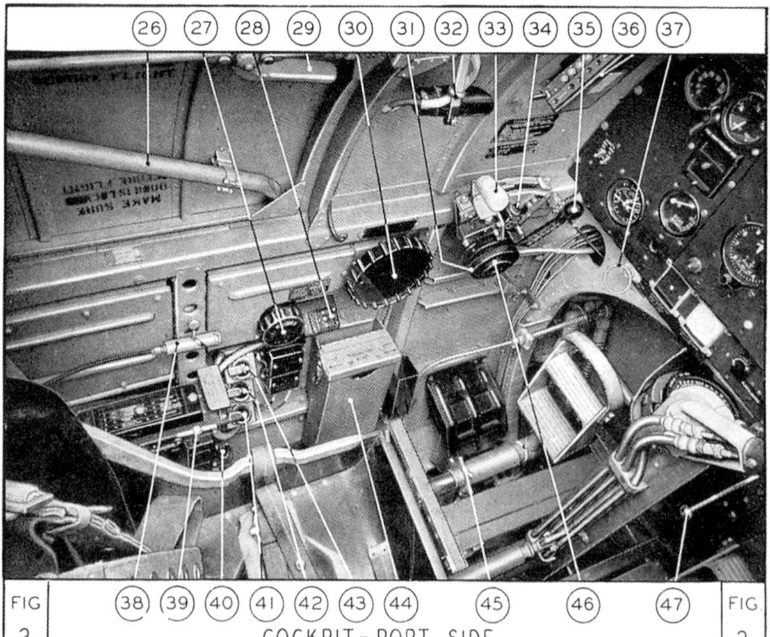

FIG 2

COCKPIT-PORT SIDE

FIG. 2

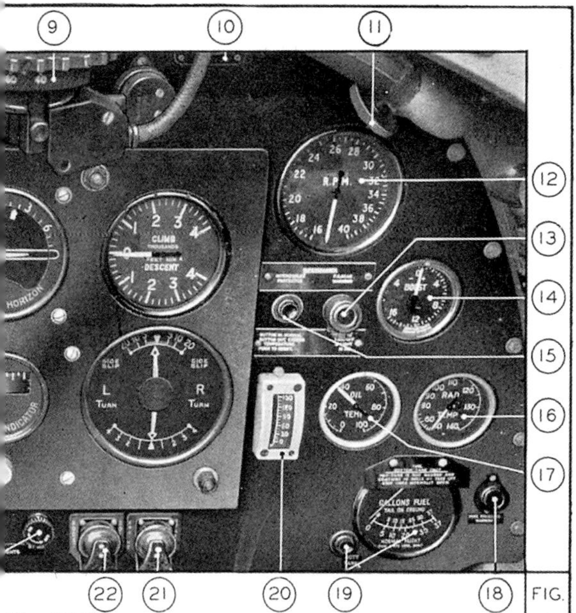

NT PANEL

FIG. 1

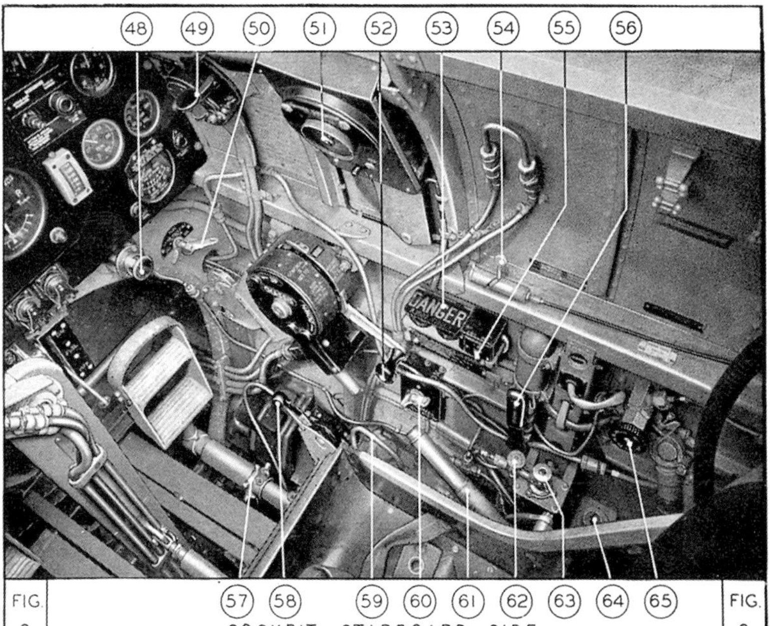

FIG. 3

COCKPIT – STARBOARD · SIDE

FIG. 3

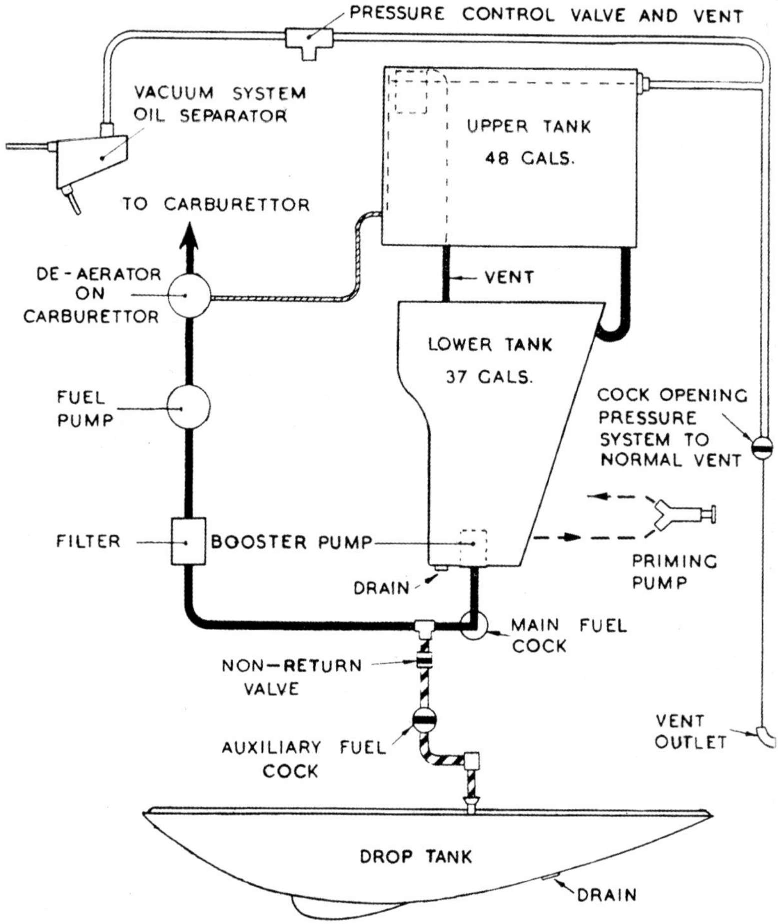

BOOSTER PUMP INSTALLATION
LATER MERLIN 66 & 70 ENGINES

MAIN FUEL SYSTEM	▬▬▬▬▬	DE-AERATOR SYSTEM	▭▭▭▭▭
AUXILIARY SYSTEM	▰▰▰▰▰	PRESSURE SYSTEM	═════
PRIMING SYSTEM	– – ▸ – –		

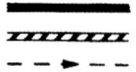

FIG 4 — FUEL SYSTE
MERLIN 61 & 63 ENGINES ARE NOT F